WESTERN

* * ★ * *

SCARVES

WESTERN

* * * ★ * * *

SCARVES

DIANE ZAMOST • PHOTOGRAPHS by **WENDY McEAHERN**

GIBBS SMITH
TO ENRICH AND INSPIRE HUMANKIND

First Edition
18 17 16 15 14   5 4 3 2 1

Published by
Gibbs Smith
P.O. Box 667
Layton, Utah 84041

1.800.835.4993 orders
www.gibbs-smith.com

Designed by mGraphicDesign
Printed and bound in Hong Kong

Gibbs Smith books are printed on either recycled,
100% post-consumer waste, FSC-certified papers or on
paper produced from sustainable PEFC-certified forest/
controlled wood source. Learn more at www.pefc.org.

Library of Congress Cataloging-in-Publication Data

Zamost, Diane.
    Western scarves / Diane Zamost ; Photographs by
Wendy McEahern. — First edition.
        p. cm.
    ISBN 978-1-4236-3618-2
1. Scarves—United States—History. 2. Scarves—United
States—Pictorial works. 3. West (U.S.) I. Title.
    GT2113.Z36 2014
    391.4'10973—dc23
                                        2013040213

★ ACKNOWLEDGMENTS

This book is dedicated to all the unknown artists and illustrators of these scarves without whom there wouldn't be a book. And to Wendy McEahern, for capturing these images so beautifully. To the singing cowboys, the poets, the balladeers, who, like the artists, keep the stories alive through songs and poetry. And, of course, the working cowboys and cowgirls, whose livelihoods and traditions, spanning nearly 150 years, inspired so much of this book.

A special thanks to Star Liana York, a sculptor and artist who very graciously gave Wendy and myself the run of her ranch for a photo shoot and access to her incredibly zen-like animals. Also to her husband, Jeff Brock, and his collection of old trucks and various parts of his racing rockets for props, and their beautiful view of the New Mexico sky and mountains. We clearly saw where all their artistic and creative inspiration stems from.

Then there are all the wonderful and colorful saddle pals along the trail: Carol Link, Brian Wright, Cheryl Lampros and "the group," Shorty Koger and the whole dang family, Claudia Laughlin, Mike Paparo, Teddi Marks, Roy Flynn, Don Seeger, Jack Pressler, Jeff and Estee Roll, Gilda Baker, James Mann, Peter D, and the entire family of cowboy trade show and antique dealers up and down the trail. All are friendships not soon forgotten.

I have to mention Tyler Beard for having said, "You should write a book about these scarves." To Gibbs Smith for saying, "Why don't you?" and to the staff at Gibbs Smith, Publisher for helping two tenderfoots, Wendy and myself, throughout this book process.

To Wily Jim Pfeiffer, the best and most versatile singing cowboy and guitar picker out there, for keeping the original western swingabilly music alive and kicking for the enjoyment of those lucky enough to hear him.

Thanks to all the ones along the way who said you could, and to all the ones who said I couldn't. Last, but by no means least, to Rising Star, my equine buddy, for the trail ride of a lifetime.

I thank you all.

CONTENTS

INTRO-DUCTION

{ "SO, WHERE DID THIS COWBOY THING COME FROM?" MY DAD ASKED, NOT LONG BEFORE HE WENT TO RIDE THE OTHER RANGE. }

IT'S BEEN SAID WE ARE ALL BORN INTO A PLACE AND TIME FOR A REASON. My place—the newly settled northern suburbs of Chicago. The time—early 1950s. Okay, not exactly cowboy country, but the West came to me through a magic box called a television. Those early days of this "new" medium will forever be impressed upon the minds of those of us who experienced them in personal and sometimes profound ways. You can guess what my way was. In the 1950s and '60s, there were more westerns than any other genre of entertainment, and they influenced a whole generation. Who didn't play cowboys and Indians, good guys and bad guys, or white hat and black hat?

Looking back, I believe it instilled in me a sense of ethics and grounding that hasn't been seen much since. And who didn't have a cowboy outfit? Mine was sent to me from Aunt Ruthie who lived in San Antonio. She had no idea what she started. The outfit was white with big red roses and green vines embroidered on the shirt and pants. It had pearl snaps on the shirt and pants pockets and a red belt. Classic! A cowgirl princess was born. I am still hunting for that now vintage outfit. I know it's out there somewhere. My look was completed by pretending my bike was a horse. The seeds were planted.

Left to my own devices at an early age, it wasn't long before I started seeking out the real horses in my area. I would walk and ride my bike miles to the stables, just to hang around and eventually trading chores for a chance to ride. Trail rides led to horse shows, which led to dude ranches, all the while I would think, "Where's all the old cowgirl and cowboy stuff? The fancy fringed gloves, the embroidered shirts? Where's the short peewee boots and colorful scarves with the images I've carried around in my head all these years? I know they're here somewhere." And they were.

I don't remember whether I saw an advertisement or if someone told me about a cowboy and Indian auction. "Auction?" I thought, "Okay, could be interesting." So off I went.

I was mesmerized by the bits, spurs, saddles, the smell of the leather, and the feel of the hand-carved, tooled grooves in the leather. All the beaded moccasins and gloves, cowgirl shirts and outfits, and blankets a girl could want! The ranch and rodeo, cowboy and cowgirl images on scarves and blankets, the geometric Indian patterns and the softness of the blankets were worn smooth by years of affection. The peewee boots with their wonderful workmanship and sexy curves from the old lasts (the wooden form the boots were built on), the underslung and stacked leather heels, the colors, stitching, and inlays were all handmade. And all were works of art.

The vintage scarves with bold, colorful graphics caught my eye. Images of cowboys and cowgirls roping, riding, chasing steers, branding cattle, bustin' broncs, singing and dancing, campfire cooking, and chuck wagons danced across the scarves. All illustrated, drawn, and originally colored by hand on silks and rayon fabrics. Seeing all the people at the

auction, also interested in vintage western stuff, made my eyes pop open!

I bought my first blankets and fancy cowgirl shirts and scarves, giggling at the excitement of finding cowgirl heaven—and in Illinois of all places! I started going to antiques shows, auctions, flea markets, trade days, anywhere I could get to on weekends, even flying a few times, to find vintage western items. Friends and acquaintances started showing an interest in my newfound obsession, wanting to know where they could get some cowgirl stuff too. "Why, right here," I thought. Wahoo! was born.

I took my collection of vintage and new cowboy and cowgirl gear and hit the road in 1993. I traveled, selling and buying along the way, to horse shows, horse expos, rodeos and ranch rodeos (big difference between the two), stock shows, western antiques shows, cowboy poetry gatherings, western music festivals, and bit and spur shows. I went everywhere I thought I'd find buyers and sellers who lived and loved a western lifestyle and appreciated antiques and collectibles. To my delight, I discovered these people were everywhere: in big cities, small towns, and all over the country.

For those of us who like to collect certain things there is no formal schooling for what we learn along the way. I learned by doing and experiencing. Some of us are lucky enough to come upon a more experienced mentor for a while, but by and large we learn as we go. A large part of it is knowledge passed around the campfire, so to speak. Heck, if you hang around other collectors and sellers long enough, something's bound to stick! And those of us blessed enough to make our way in this world, surrounding ourselves with the things we love, fueling the passions that keep us going—well, what can be more cowboy and American than that?

It's amazing what you can discover and find out in this world when you take that leap of faith and do what you love. The opportunities; the doors that open along the way; and the wonderful, fun, down-to-earth, hard-working people whom I've met along the way have been nothing short of amazing in so many ways. In time, I moved to Weatherford, Texas, and then on to Santa Fe, New Mexico. God bless Texas, but high and dry Santa Fe can spoil a gal. Nowadays I spend most of my time in the shop here in Santa Fe, still selling, buying, and collecting vintage scarves, boots, blankets, jewelry, and other cowboy collectibles and memorabilia from the "golden age." I feel like I'm just getting started!

I wrote this book to document the illustrative artwork of vintage western scarves. It's a visual book to evoke a feeling, a mood, a sense of fun and excitement, of freedom, individuality, spirit, passion, and romance. It's a result from my own interest in the West and in western cowboy culture and couture. The lifestyle these images speak of through depictions of ranch life, rodeos, dude ranches, and singing cowboys is uniquely American. Here are stories, activities, and memories that have captured our imaginations for generations and will continue to do so.

It should be said that I use the word *cowboy,* with no reference to gender, to mean cowgirls too. I've seen as many cowgirls as cowboys put in a hard day's work and do it better! Also, to me, vintage means more than fifty years old. At the time of this writing, that means the 1960s and back. So something from the '80s is not to be mistaken for vintage. With our modern busy lifestyles, our cowboy pioneering spirit has been put up for awhile. It's my hope that the images and words in this book rekindle a passion, which has always been there. As you turn the pages, I hope a nostalgic smile comes to your face. Thanks for reading and enjoy the ride.

❋

{ ...SURROUNDING OURSELVES WITH THE THINGS WE LOVE, FUELING THE PASSIONS THAT KEEP US GOING—WELL, WHAT CAN BE MORE COWBOY AND AMERICAN THAN THAT? }

I BOUGHT MY FIRST BLANKETS
AND FANCY COWGIRL SHIRTS
AND SCARVES, GIGGLING AT
THE EXCITEMENT OF FINDING
COWGIRL HEAVEN.

THE HISTORY OF THE COWBOY SCARF

WHEN IT CAME TO A COWBOY'S OUT-FIT, EVERYTHING HAD A PURPOSE. From the hat on top to the boots on bottom and everything in between, it all started as protection from the elements, riding horse-back, or other utilitarian purposes.

The scarf—that seemingly lowly square of fabric—was the most versatile article of the cowboy's clothing. It hung in a convenient place, around his neck. He was never without it, and he always knew where it was. The scarf was usually folded in half, making a large triangle with the two furthest ends tied loosely in a square knot at the back of the neck with the remainder draped down the front of the chest.

It kept the sun off a cowboy's neck, especially before shirt collars came into use. When pulled up over the nose and face, it served as protection from dust kicked up by horses and cattle, especially when riding drag (behind the herd). He could wrap and carry biscuits, strain water from a muddy water hole, and wrap it over his hat and around his chin to keep it on in high wind. In freezing weather, the scarf kept his ears from getting frostbite. When washing his face in the creek, his towel was right there.

A scarf could provide first aid on the trail, becoming a bandage in a pinch or even a tourniquet or sling. The cowboy could blindfold a skittish horse or use the bandana as a hobble. It could be used as a piggin' string to tie a calf's legs or as a rag to hold a hot branding iron. And like a yanked-off piece of leather fringe, it's a temporary fix on busted tack.

These old silks are generally known as "Pendleton Rodeo" scarves after the famous Pendleton Rodeo they are originally from. Dated from the 1920s through the '40s, these thin, wispy scarves are unique for their hand-sewn borders with images of cowboys roping on horseback, Indians, cattle, and geometric symbols. A lot of these scarves were bought in bulk quantities by the rodeos and were either hand-stamped or silk-screened with the name of the event they promoted.

Why, he could even handcuff a horse thief or cattle rustler should the need arise.

Easily rinsed and washed, scarves could be used over and over again. Many a gal fashioned one from her dress fabric to give to her beau as a gentle reminder from whence he came and to whom he should return. You can almost see him, gazing at the moon and stars, gently running his fingers across the fabric, and dreaming of a softer pillow! How many fights must've broke out over a missing or misplaced scarf?

In the rodeo arena, bright colors were and still are the order of the day—the brighter the better. Out riding the range, however, muted colors were generally preferred. Especially in the early days of the open range since drawing attention from a distance was not desired. Many a cowboy of days gone by believed that bright colors could spook the cattle or horses. Whatever the regional style, be it Great Basin or Northwest buckaroo, Southwest or California, Texas or Montana, the cowboy in the American West was rarely without a scarf.

Through the years these large squares of cotton, silk, rayon, or what have you, have been referred to by a number of different names. They've been called neckerchiefs, scarves, bandanas, wipes, mufflers, wild rags, and handkerchiefs. Nowadays, many of us are more specific with our descriptions. Handkerchiefs are usually 12 x 12 inches, bandanas 18 to 24 inches square, neckerchiefs usually fall into the bandana size range, and wild rags are 36 x 36 but can now be had in 42-inch-square.

Although cowboy scarves and bandanas started as a necessity along the trail in the mid- and late-1800s, as time went on they became popular souvenir items for those adventurous souls traveling through the West. They were used as an advertising medium and sold as souvenirs of Wild West shows, rodeos, Route 66 curio shops, national parks, round-ups, state fairs, Fred Harvey hotels, and guest and dude ranches. The iconic bucking horse and rider being the most popular and recognizable symbol of the

THESE LARGE SQUARES OF COTTON, SILK, RAYON, OR WHAT HAVE YOU, HAVE BEEN REFERRED TO BY A NUMBER OF DIFFERENT NAMES. THEY'VE BEEN CALLED NECKERCHIEFS, SCARVES, BANDANAS, WIPES, MUFFLERS, WILD RAGS, AND HANDKERCHIEFS.

Royal Gorge Colo

West and all the adventure it had to offer. The scarves became commercially manufactured, and a promoter could print the name of a rodeo or event onto the fabric and they were in business. I wish it were that easy now!

They were, and still are, perfect for the traveler as they take up almost no room in a suitcase and can be folded up and put in a pocket. But it's no coincidence that the popularity of cowboy scarves and western wear in general exploded with the rise of the stylized Hollywood singing cowboy, who first appeared on the silver screen in the 1920s. And what a dandy this singing, guitar strumming, rope twirling, horse rider became! In the 1940s and '50s, the scarf exploded in detail with complicated and wildly colorful graphics. It was as if the artists and illustrators couldn't cram enough images onto a piece of fabric. Rayons and acetates became the fabrics of choice as silk was needed for parachutes and such during the war efforts of the '40s. This was the heyday of the best artwork on cowboy scarves. These pieces are highly suitable for framing and display, with their vibrant pops of color and hand-drawn graphics—and even

One of the best illustrations of a rodeo bronc rider I've seen and an example of a rodeo stamping their name on ready-made scarves.

history and geography lessons on some!

Who were these artists? After spending some time searching, I've come up empty-handed. They probably worked for the companies who made the scarves, never signing their work, never being recognized for their talents except for a steady paycheck. The quality of these scarves and all vintage pieces is unequaled in today's market of mass-produced, computer driven, throwaway items we're surrounded with. Manufacturers today do reproduce some of the old designs, but they're so often missing the feel of the fabric, workmanship, and hand-drawn graphics of old. The vintage pieces have soul, passion, and a story to tell, which is why they endure today.

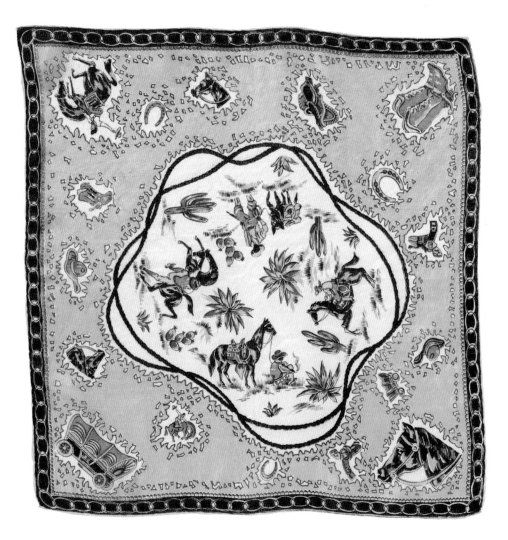

It's not unusual to see the same scarves in different colors. These small, thin, silk examples date from the 1930s to the mid-40s.

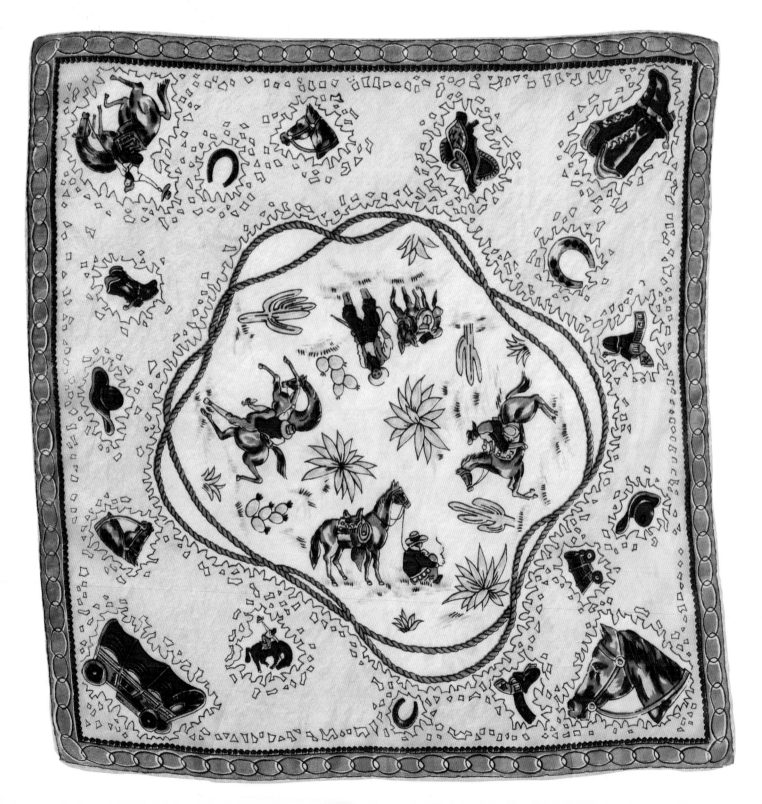

THE QUALITY OF
THESE SCARVES
AND ALL
VINTAGE PIECES
IS UNEQUALED IN
TODAY'S MARKET.

The Old Chisholm Trail undated
*"I woke up one morning on the old Chisholm Trail
With a rope in my hand and a cow by the tail
Com-a ti- yi-yip-pee yip-pee yea, yip-pee yea,
Com-a ti-yi- yip-pee yip-pee yea!"*

← I've had a few personal favorites over the years. This one ranks at the top. This vintage piece features the obligatory bucking horse in bright colors. It also has some very famous ranch brands scattered throughout its great design: the 6666, The XIT, the much-marketed Flying W brand, the Pitchfork Ranch brand, Lazy 8, Rocking W, and OK ranch, among others. Most of the ranches on this scarf are still operating today as working cattle and horse ranches.

It also includes a fancy hat, saddle, spurs, and boots. Cowboys and cowgirls hanging out on fences, and hand-rolling and smoking cigarettes (Oh my!). It has large rope lettering exclaiming, "Let 'er go." An old tag on it reads, "10 momme," which is a reference to the weight of the silk; "Brico," apparently the company who made it; and "pure silk." The hem has a very fine machine serge. Brico scarfs were made in Japan in the 1950s and '60s. Whether or not Brico was a Japan-based company or an American company that had scarves made in Japan is unclear.

· · · · ·

↑ Another scarf celebrating the cowboy bronc rider, but rarely is seen a vintage scarf with a woman riding bucking horses or broncs. This acrylic fabric scarf dates from the 1950s.

ART OF THE DUDE RANCH

STARTING IN THE LATE 1800S, THE RAILROADS BROUGHT PEOPLE WESTWARD ON VACATIONS. First they came to the national parks and then to the guest ranches that sprung up around the parks. With the region being settled, it was finally safe to "go West" without fear of losing life and limb. Off the train, the wagon would meet you at the station to take you to your destination guest ranch. Your experience could be as rustic or opulent as you were willing to pay for, which led to some of these western resorts becoming known as playgrounds for the rich. Travel was expensive and time-consuming back then, so guests would stay for weeks at a time or even all summer.

No boots? No jeans? No problem. You could get outfitted at the ranch. They sold everything you needed. They still do.

Scarves were the perfect souvenirs for the guys and gals to take home, both for bragging rights of their great time and as remembrances. Dude and guest ranch scenes were a popular theme on cowboy scarves. With images of roping, riding, branding, singing cowboys, dancing, and wranglers on bucking broncs, they helped to romanticize the West and promote tourism.

The guest ranches had a special appeal to young society ladies. Away from a controlled big city environment, they were more able to do as they pleased. A dude ranch was very democratic for those early days. Women wore jeans and boots, just like the men, and nobody looked twice. A woman was expected to pull her own weight and saddle her own horse, so to speak. She may do some chores, clean a corral or two, or water the livestock. For some, it might have been their first feeling of freedom. She could wake with the dawn in the cool crispness of a western morning, and head to the corral to be greeted with a nicker from her favorite horse, the warm breath mixing with the cool morning air. Saddling up her pal, she could hop on and head out, hitting the trail and listening to the rhythmic sound of the hooves. With the clean smell of the morning air and the peacefulness and quiet, it was heaven on earth.

Cowboys and cowgirls hanging out and flirtin' round the ol' corral.

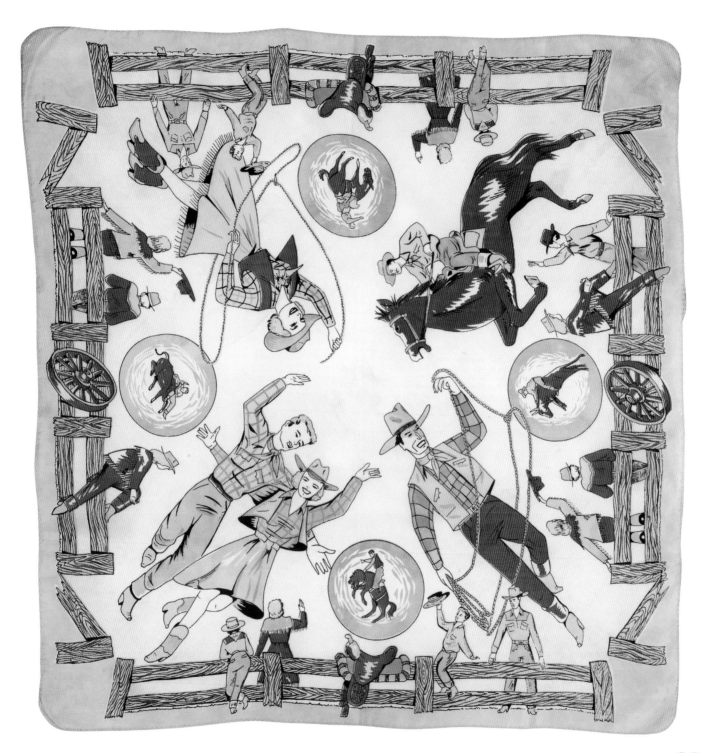

39

Many a cowgirl, young and old, has left a piece of her heart behind at a dude ranch. (And not because of a cowboy. Although I'm sure a little ranch romance was common as well.) One rarely left unchanged.

Today, a dude ranch vacation is still one of the best experiences one can have at any age. There are different kinds of horse activities and events to suit every taste and experience level. There are also cattle drives, hayrides, chuck wagon suppers, campfires, singing cowboys, and dances. A guest can pan for gold, swim, go whitewater rafting, fly fish, and canoe. Some guest ranches are family oriented and others are for adults. Some have amenities that rival the best resorts with gourmet dining and world-class spas. So take the kids, or yourself, and leave the gadgets at home. Unwind and relax, you won't regret it. The old adage, "The outside of a horse is good for the inside of a man," still rings true.

＊

Annie get your gun.

45

47

→ Ropin' Cowboy Rag c. 1996
Wily Western Music BMI
Wily Jim Pfeiffer (Used by permission)
"Can he really ride and rope just like a real live cowboy / You can bet your boots that boy don't fool around / Twist and twirl and skip it too, watch him now boys / He ain't too tied up to go to town."
. . . . .

→ Singing cowboys are a familiar sight at any dude ranch and really add to the western experience. Ain't nothing like sitting around a campfire and being serenaded by a good lookin' cowboy. And they're all good lookin' cowboys. I wouldn't visit a ranch without one.

"THE OUTSIDE OF A HORSE IS GOOD FOR THE INSIDE OF A MAN."

A cowboy's accouterments: hats, saddles, saddle bags, guns, rifles, holsters, bits, spurs, ropes, branding irons, banjo guitars, horseshoes, and first place ribbons.

↑ *"Swing your partner round and round."*

. . . . .

→ Perfect dude ranch-style: a leather fringed jacket and a scarf around your neck.

· · · ★ · · ·

STATE
OF THE
SCARF

{ EACH STATE SCARF
HIGHLIGHTS TOURIST
ATTRACTIONS, POINTS
OF INTEREST, THINGS
TO DO AND SEE,
AND IN THE WEST,
COWBOYS. }

ABOUT EVERY STATE HAS HAD A STATE SOUVENIR SCARF AT ONE TIME OR ANOTHER. I've seen them depicted in old photos as far back as the 1920s. The ones from the western states naturally had images of cowboys and ranching activities. As with every good advertising campaign, each state had its own slogan printed. Montana had "Land of Shining Mountains" and "The Treasure State." Wyoming was "Wonderful Wyoming." Texas had "The Lone Star State." Colorado, "Colorful Colorado" and "Colorado, the Centennial State." Arizona seems to set a record of sorts by claiming, "Colorful Arizona Kingdom of the Sun," "Land of Fun and Sun," and "The Grand Canyon State." California is "The Golden State" and Oklahoma, "The Sooner State."

New Mexico was called "The Sunshine State" in the earlier silk scarves until Florida trademarked that slogan, so then New Mexico became "The Land of Enchantment." Even one South Dakota scarf called itself "The Sunshine State." Each state scarf highlights tourist attractions, points of interest, things to do and see, and in the West, cowboys.

Some scarves highlighted the seventeen western states, depicting the rodeo towns in each state. Along with some misspelling of towns, are colorful images of bucking horses, roping and riding cowboys along with all their accouterments like branding irons, spurs, hats, saddles, ropes, and boots. Indians on horseback, along with other Native American images like teepees, bows and arrows, and Indian chiefs in full headdress also appeared on these scarves. I suppose some poor ol' rodeo contestant could've used one of these scarves as a sort of road map should he happen to be bounced on his head one too many times to remember how to get to the next rodeo. "Cause there's always the next rodeo."

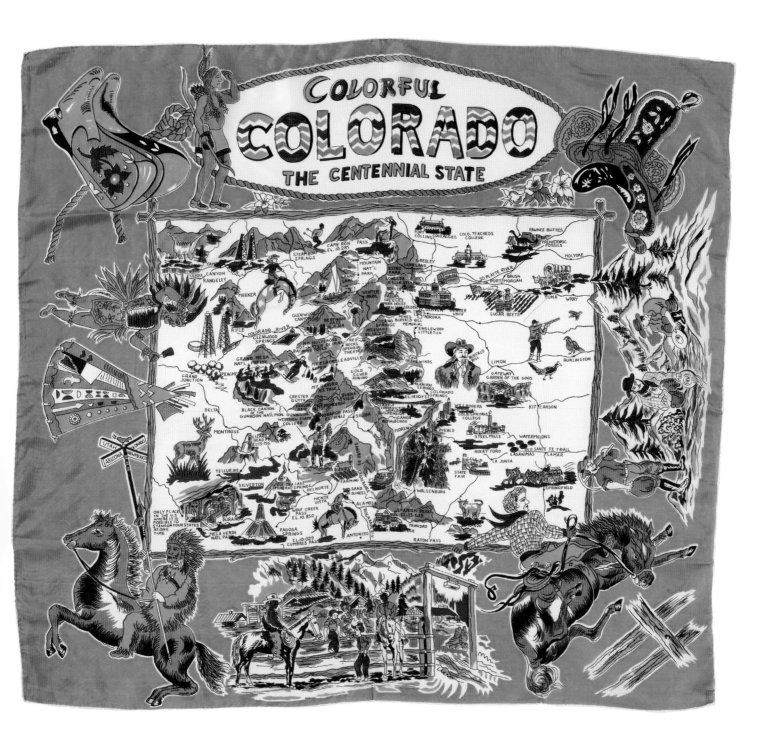

63

**I'd Like To Be In Texas When
They Round Up In The Spring** c. 1916
Carl Copeland
*"I can see the cattle grazing o'er the hills
at early morn / I can see the campfires
smoking at the breaking of the dawn /
I can hear the bronco's neighing, I can
hear the cowboy sing / I'd like to be in
Texas for the roundup in the spring."*

71

73

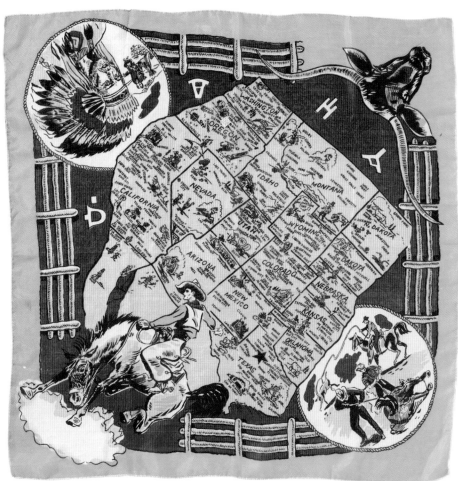

↑ Native Americans were usually shown in full headdress. This silk, western states scarf dates from the 1930s to the mid-40s.

SOME POOR OL' RODEO CONTESTANT COULD'VE USED ONE OF THESE SCARVES AS A SORT OF ROAD MAP TO GET TO THE NEXT RODEO. "CAUSE THERE'S ALWAYS THE NEXT RODEO."

Ragtime Cowboy Joe c. 1912 / Grant Clarke

"He always sings / Raggy music to the cattle / As he swings / Back and forward in the saddle / On a horse / that's a syncopated gaiter / There's-a such a funny meter / To the roar of his repeater. / How they run / When they hear his gun / Because the Western folks all know / He's a highfalutin, rootin', shootin', / Son of a gun from Arizona, / Ragtime Cowboy Joe."

ARIZONA SEEMS TO SET A RECORD OF SORTS BY CLAIMING, "COLORFUL ARIZONA KINGDOM OF THE SUN," "LAND OF FUN AND SUN," AND "THE GRAND CANYON STATE."

← Looks like this rayon 1950s Oklahoma state scarf was made to match the paint job, or was it the other way around?

ROCKABILLY: SOMETHING OLD SOMETHING NEW

THE TERM "ROCKABILLY" COMES FROM A BLEND OF ROCK 'N' ROLL AND HILLBILLY MUSIC. It's a precursor to the rock music we know today. Other strong musical influences include western swing, jump blues, swingabilly, boogie woogie, and rhythm and blues.

Early recording artists of this music include the Maddox Brothers and Rose, a very early Elvis Presley, Johnny Cash, and Carl Perkins (all three of these young fellows recorded for Sun Records in Memphis in the 1950s). Then there's Wanda Jackson (still touring in her eighties), Eddie Cochran, Jerry Lee Lewis, Buddy Holly, and others too numerous to list. Newer generations have latched onto a contemporary resurgence of this music.

Rockabilly today can include a lifestyle and a style of dress, which is a western and swing combination from the 1940s and '50s. The guys have pompadour hairstyles and pomade. They want vintage everything: cowboy shirts, denim with jeans rolled up just so, cowboy boots and engineer's (motorcycle) boots, western belts and buckles, and scarves. They want the real deal. They wear vintage when they can find it—and fit into it. In the 1940s and '50s, people were considerably smaller than the average size today. The same dress goes for the gals, but also includes vintage swing dresses and all the accessories that go with them. Think Marlon Brando's *The Wild One* or James

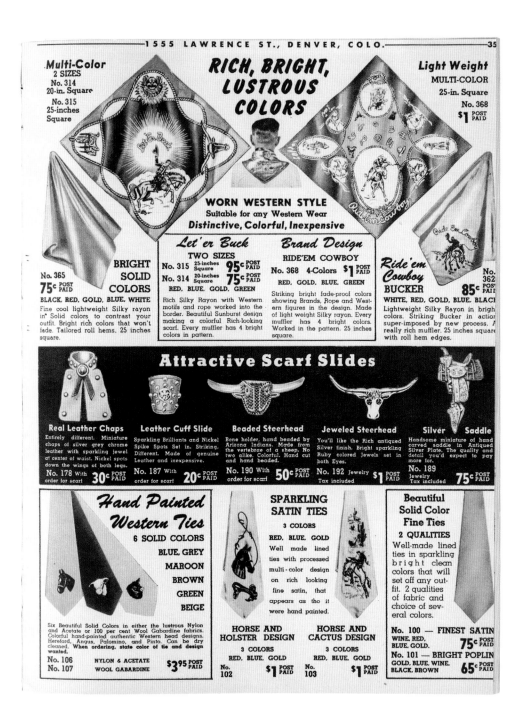

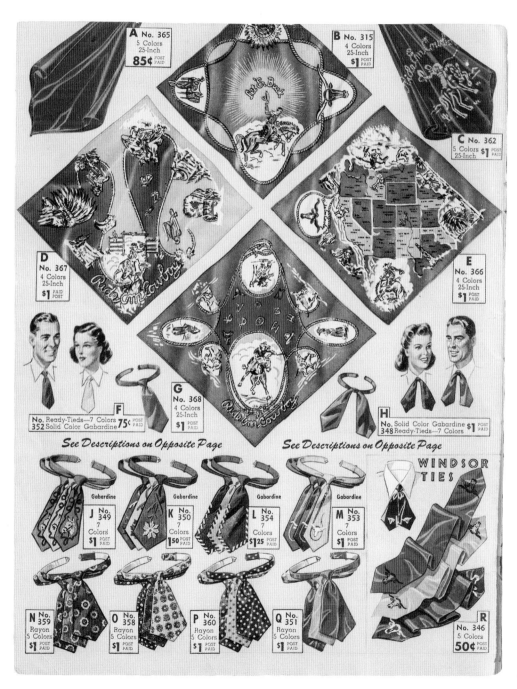

Dean's *Rebel Without a Cause* mixed with cowboy and swing style.

Rockabilly is a step back in time with a modern twist, and part of that modern twist is "ink" or tattoos. Tats can be as alarming to parents as James Dean's portrayals of rebellion were in his day. Every generation and movement has its own thing. They also love to dance and swing to the rockabilly music. They love vintage cars and hot rods. Yes, hot rods and street rods beautifully and lovingly restored.

This resurgence is big in the United States, but it's huge in Europe, Sweden, and the United Kingdom, with various rockabilly festivals and gatherings across the globe. Las Vegas has one every April called Rockabilly

Weekend. People come from all over the world for a long weekend of dancing to great live music, a hot rod car show, various activities like dance contests and lessons, a burlesque show and competition, a vintage fashion show, tiki pool party, tattoo lounge, and shopping from vendors who cater to their vintage rockabilly lifestyle. Check out www.vivalasvegas.net for more info and tickets. It's known to sell out. There are also other smaller gatherings that pop up from time to time.

This rockabilly movement is a new take on western and cowboy lifestyle. Is it different? Yes. Take some getting used to? You bet, for some. But what doesn't change and evolve? The horse aspect is a little lacking, but it's just a different kind of horsepower. I love when these rockabillies come into the store, decked out in their vintage cowboy and swing outfits, on their way to or from Vegas, traveling Route 66. They don't all speak English, but the reassuring nod makes me glad to see western influences continuing and gaining new fans across the world. Long may it live. Wahoo!

In the 1950s and '60s, cotton bandanas such as these colorful examples were sold by the thousands in boxed sets with everything a little buckaroo needed to be outfitted: spurs, six-shooters with holsters, chaps, a sheriff badge, and, of course, a cotton scarf. No self-respecting little cowpoke's outfit was complete without one.

95

Cotton-fringed scarves like this one were also popular as dresser and table toppers, as well as wearing pieces. I've found them square- and rectangular-shaped. This one dates from the 1950s.

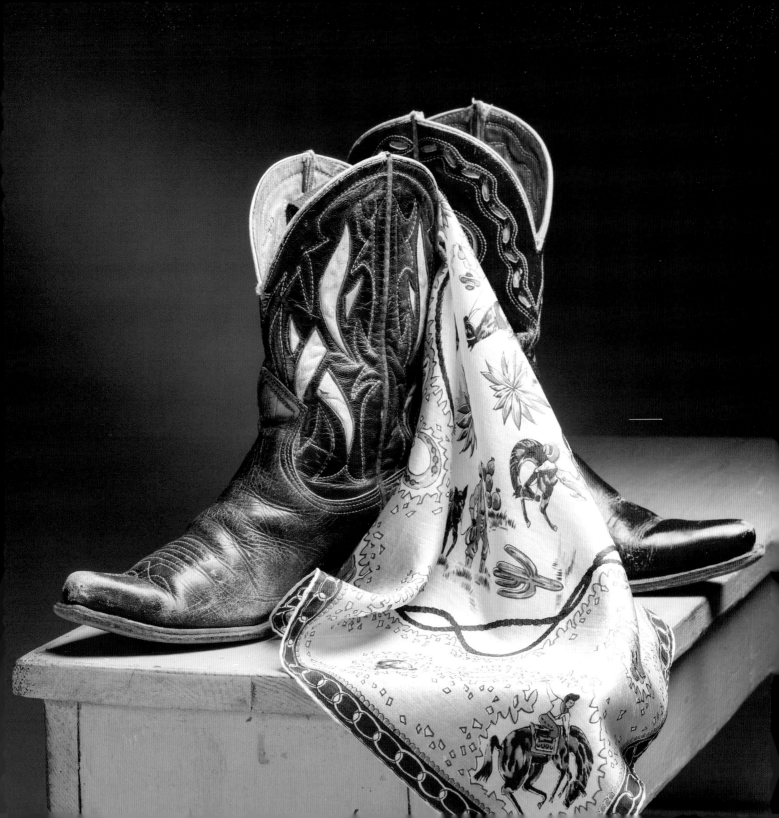

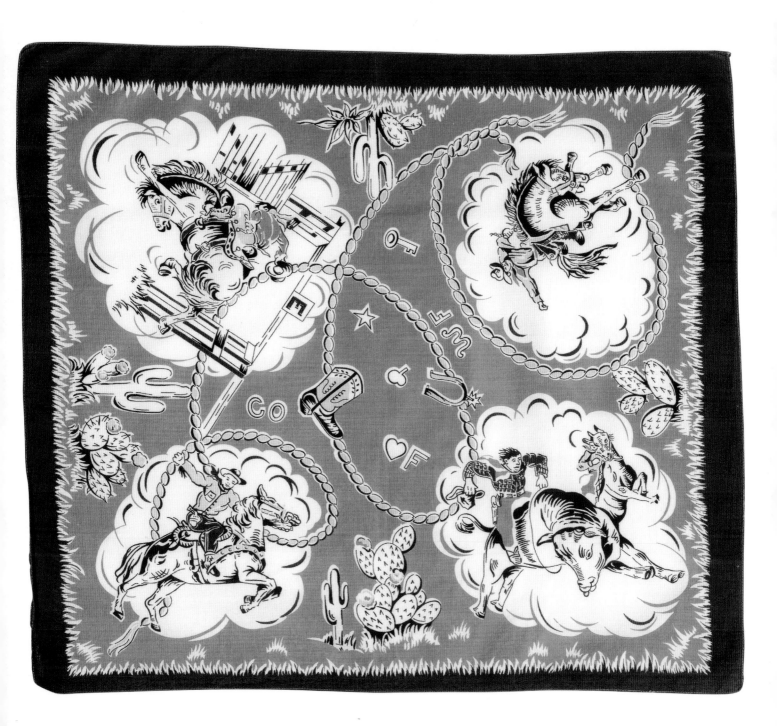

99

CONTEMPORARY ARTISTS' SCARVES

★

TODAY, THERE ARE SOME GREAT WESTERN ARTISTS PRODUCING AND REPRODUCING THEIR ARTWORK ONTO SILK SCARVES. Most are large wild-rag size, 35-inch-square, great for wearing and wonderful for framing. Artists each have their own style, of course, and bring their own vision of the West to these unique scarves. They've made for some beautiful artwork.

{ TO SEE A SKILLED BUCKAROO THROW A BIG LOOP RIATA IS TRULY A THING OF BEAUTY AS IT GRACEFULLY SAILS THROUGH THE AIR. }

BUCKEYE BLAKE

Buckeye's use of brilliant colors enhances his bold, vintage artistic style. He lives what he paints. Even though he lives in Texas now, his Northwest buckaroo influence shines through. His art shows a nice blending of the buckaroo and Texas cowboy.

The differences between a buckaroo and a cowboy stemmed originally from where they lived. Over the years the lines have been blurred, but these are the basics when it comes to their clothing.

A buckaroo-style hat is typically a flat crown with a wide, flat brim. The cowboy will be inclined towards a rancher's or cattlemen's crease for the crown with the brim curved up on the sides.

Both now wear wild rags, although it was a buckaroo custom first. Buckaroo shirts are buttoned with no pockets and have small round collars versus the popular snap shirts of cowboys with pockets. Cowboys prefer belts, but a buckaroo likes suspenders. When it comes to boots, cowboys tend to a shorter style, while a buckaroo will wear tall boots, often with the pants tucked in. A buckaroo is usually more stylish in terms of dress and equipment.

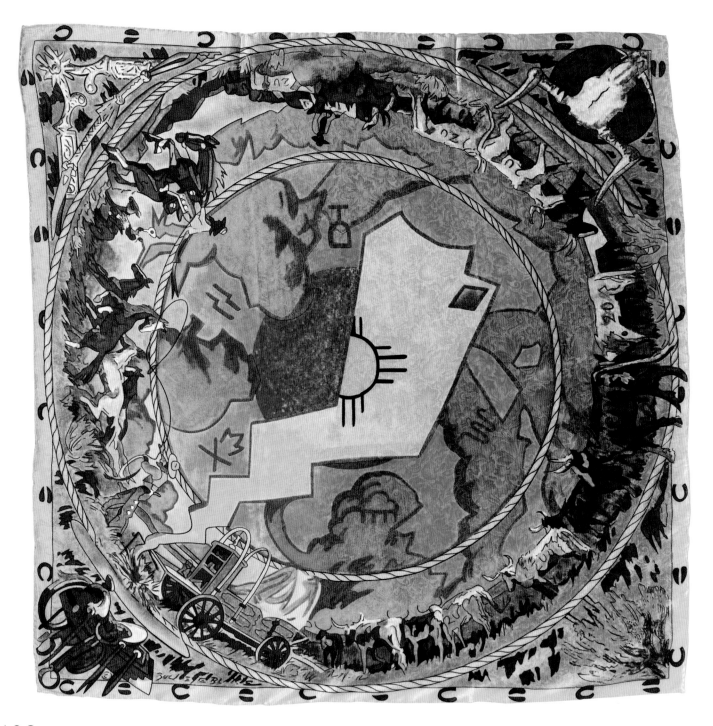

TEAL BLAKE

In contrast to his father, Buckeye, Teal's style is softer, more delicate looking. His use of watercolors on the scarves reflects his other works of art. However, like his father, he lives what he paints in Texas.

DAVID HOLL

Dave, a buckaroo artist, has only done artwork for one scarf, but what a beauty. Drawn in charcoal, the scarf has images of the buckaroo-style cowboys of the Northwest with their flat-crowned, wide-brim hats, long big loop riatas, and bosal and hackamore bridles. To see a skilled buckaroo throw a big loop riata is truly a thing of beauty as it gracefully sails through the air. Dave is now in Arizona and spends most of his time ranching.

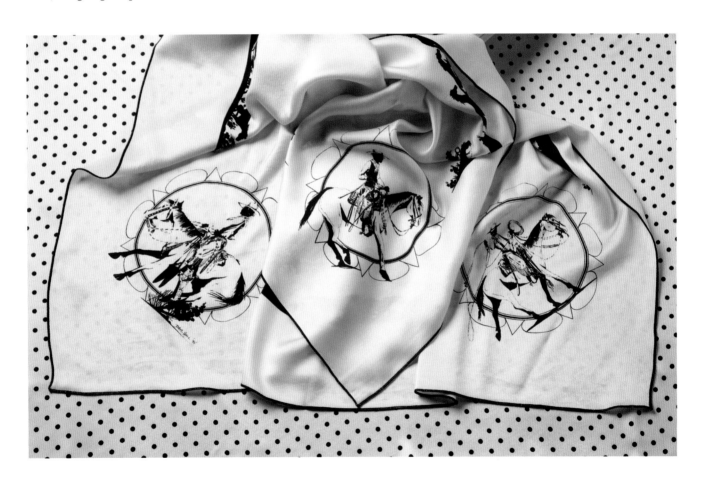

111

DONNA HOWELL-SICKLES

Donna paints happy, smiling, red-lipsticked cowgirls proudly wearing their scarves and waving their hats. They always look like they're having fun. Who wouldn't? They're always surrounded by things cowgirls love: horses, dogs, cattle, and in the example shown here, their cowboy boots. Donna has done an entire series of her artwork on scarves and other gift items that embrace the cowgirl spirit.

113

JOELLE SMITH

Joelle painted what she saw and, lucky for us, she saw a lot. In her too-short time on this range, she created an impressive collection of works of cowboys, buckaroos, horses, dogs, chickens, brandings, and round-ups. She personally knew a lot of her subjects, if not all of them. Her images make you feel like you're right there, observing yourself. I especially love her floral borders and her "punchy" buckaroo looks. She is missed.

TYING ONE ON
AND OTHER USES

WESTERN SCARVES HAVE COME A LONG WAY FROM THEIR HUMBLE BEGINNINGS as a simple but versatile and utilitarian item to the highfalutin world of fashion. There are various ways of tying one on and using and displaying them. Below are a few of the more popular ways.

The most popular way for both men and women to wear them is around the neck, tied in various knots or with a scarf slide. Scarf slides come in a variety of shapes and sizes, but a handy one can be fashioned from a ring. Take a square-shaped scarf, fold it into a triangle, place the V of the triangle down the back of the neck, and slip the slide onto the two ends in the front.

← These vintage remake scarves with slides were a joint venture between Alan Chadwick and myself. They were limited editions and sold out a few years back.

The gals can also fashion them into head wraps. Gypsy or turban style is popular, or tied under the chin like my mom used to do so she wouldn't mess her "do" when she put the top down on her car. Anyone can also tie it around the waist with the V draped over one hip and tied in a knot over the other hip. Put it through your belt loops on a pair of jeans or belted over a dress.

I've used them as a carry-all bag, hobo-style, like when you used to pretend you were running away from home as a kid down the block to your friend's house. Put your stuff in the center of the scarf and tie up the opposite corners. Stick is optional.

They look great displayed in the house, laid over the back of an upholstered chair, sofa, or over a lamp. Lay it on a dresser to keep your pocket change and jewelry from scratching the top of the wood or turn them into eye-catching pillows.

I'VE USED THEM AS A CARRY-ALL BAG, HOBO-STYLE . . . PUT YOUR STUFF IN THE CENTER OF THE SCARF AND TIE UP THE OPPOSITE CORNERS. STICK IS OPTIONAL.

My favorite thing to do with these vintage scarves, and the best way to appreciate the great artwork, is to frame them. Have the scarf mounted square- or diamond-shaped in the frame (whichever way suits the piece best). It makes for an impressive presentation that looks great on the wall or leaning against the back of a bookshelf. Instant western style!

Scarves will need to be pressed from time to time—especially before framing—to get the wrinkles out. It is best to press them as opposed to ironing. Start with a medium-heat range and spray with water from a spray bottle that has been adjusted for a wide spray. Take the iron and press down on the fabric for about 3 to 5 seconds. Lift the iron. Are the wrinkles gone? If so, it's the right heat level. If not, turn the heat up a bit and try again. The heavier the fabric, the longer it will take. Don't be shy about repeating the process as needed.

If you're storing your scarves for a period of time, fold gently and place in a clean, unused gallon food storage plastic bag. Do not press all the air out before zipping the bag closed. Keeping a little air in the bag helps to keep the fabric from crushing. The plastic bag also keeps any little gnawing critters at bay.

Here are some step-by-step instructions for tying some popular knots. They all start out the same, with the scarf folded into a triangle, with the triangle V in the back and the two ends hanging in the front. For a tighter fit that keeps your neck warmer when riding the range in colder climates, put the V of the triangle in the front, take the two ends and crisscross it behind the neck, bringing the ends back to the front. The ends are now ready to tie in the knot of your choosing or use a slide.

→ Sometimes I find these great old pieces with the tag still attached. This one reads, "pure silk, hand-rolled, made in Japan."

THE BIB KNOT

Step 1: Fold the scarf into a triangle.

Step 2: Tie knot in one folded end, forming a loop.

Step 3: Pull other folded end through loop and tighten.

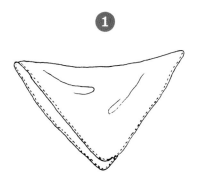

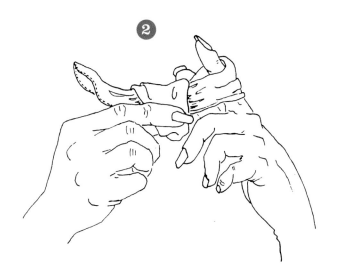

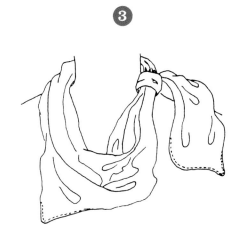

➔ The Bib Knot appears on a vintage scarf.

THE SLIDING KNOT

Step 1: Hold the scarf taut with your right hand while using your other hand to bring one end over the top of the opposite end.

Step 2: Let go of the left hand and grab the same end from behind the fabric and bring it back across the top to the opposite side.

Step 3: With your right hand, take the end behind the fabric, go over the top, and push the end through the loop that was made in step 2.

OK, you've got this one mastered. Now it's time to head on over into the big leagues, to the grand daddy of 'em all— the Buckaroo Square Knot.

→ The Sliding Knot appears on a vintage remake scarf.

THE (NOW FAMOUS) BUCKAROO SQUARE KNOT

Warning: Learning to tie this knot can lead to frustration and the occasional unintentional burst of anger at a loved one. Before attempting to learn the Buckaroo Square Knot, please warn all household members of your intention to master this knot. It's gonna take some getting used to, coordinating your fingers to hold the ends down and wrap it around. I've found doing it in front of a mirror instead of looking down on your chest is helpful. It took me three days to master, taking time off for the frustration level to subside. But, once mastered, you can tie it front ways, backwards, upside down, as well as on someone else. I guarantee the satisfaction and envy of all your friends alone will be well worth your efforts and cost of this book.

This Buckaroo Square Knot is not to be confused with the boy scout square knot you may have learned as a kid, which is the ol' right over left, left over right. This is a different animal entirely.

OK, here we go . . .

You will require a wild rag size scarf, 35-square-inches or larger, to accommodate all the wrapping around. Fingers will be referred to as fingers 1 and 2, which are the index and middle finger and fingers 3 and 4, which are the ring finger and your pinky finger.

Step 1: Fold the scarf into a triangle, and place behind your head so the two ends are hanging down the front of your chest. Using your right hand, make a loop around fingers 1 and 2. You will be using fingers 3 and 4 to hold down the end of your loop.

Step 2: While holding down the end of the loop with fingers 3 and 4, with your left hand grab the other end of the scarf and put it under your first loop, across your chest so it sits on top, slightly away from the chest. It should be at the top of the first loop that fingers 1 and 2 are still holding but under the fabric that fingers 3 and 4 are holding.

Step 3: With your left hand, pull the scarf end all the way behind your right hand, bringing it back across your chest, the opposite way. It should go behind the scarf knot in progress.

Step 4: Push the scarf end through the loop of scarf that is still being held by fingers 1 and 2 on top of the fabric that fingers 3 and 4 that are still holding.

Step 5: Your finished scarf should look like this, if knot (pun intended), repeat.

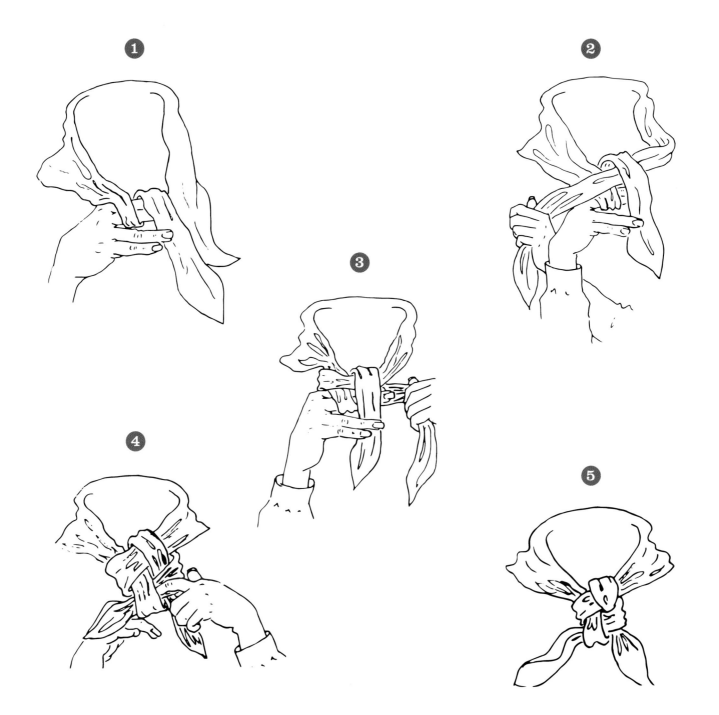

Thanks to Carla Liesen for first introducing me, and many others, to this great-looking knot. Also, I would greatly appreciate when upon ever meeting me in person, you do not express your opinion of these instructions using finger number 2.

✳

WESTERN
SCARVES HAVE
COME A LONG
WAY FROM
THEIR HUMBLE
BEGINNINGS AS
A SIMPLE BUT
VERSATILE AND
UTILITARIAN
ITEM TO THE
HIGHFALUTIN
WORLD OF FASHION.

➔ The Buckaroo Square Knot appears on a vintage remake scarf.

EPILOGUE: ROMANCE OF THE WEST

OUR ONGOING LOVE AFFAIR WITH THE WEST IS FASCINATING TO ME. I think the expansive visions of the wide-open spaces help to stretch our minds and imaginations to think of the "what-ifs?" in life and the possibilities. Just the ability to see a horizon sixty miles away and a big sky with clouds that appear as though you could reach up and touch them clears your head and provides for a peaceful timeout. I can look at an image of a cowboy on horseback and be transported to another place. I feel the need to escape, and I believe others do too.

There's an entire industry dedicated to keeping the romance of the West alive. And it would not exist if it were not for mankind's wanderlust, thrill for adventure, and hope for better things ahead. It's kept alive in movies and television, music, poetry, books, and clothing. Even you, reading these words and looking at the cowboy scarves and their printed images, help keep this going. And I, for one, thank you for that. Travel and vacation destinations, the horse and livestock industries, museums, and western lifestyle magazines all contribute. Clothing and accessories designers all over the world are also keeping it alive. A special nod and thanks to Ralph Lauren, whom I tip my big ol' cowboy hat to, for his ongoing western influence in his fashion empire.

I don't expect our ongoing romance with the West to go away anytime soon. In fact, I think it's growing. I've met cowboys, tourists, and travelers from all over the world whose enthusiasm and appetite for all things western is evident as soon as they walk into my shop. Ranging from collectors who come in pursuit of western memorabilia to take back to their country to resell, to the casual tourist who wants a souvenir or cowboy boots to wear and remind themselves of a trip to the West, they've all come to experience in some way the personal images they carry of this impressive part of the country and the history and lifestyles liberally scattered across it. The romance of the West has become a multi-billion-dollar industry, which I think is OK.

REFERENCES & CREDITS

Alan Chadwick
wyomingtraders.com

Buckeye Blake
theblakestudios.com

Donna Howell-Sickles
donnahowellsickles.com

Jeff Brock
rocketheadsstudio.com

Joelle Smith
joellesmith.com

Perspectives Fine Art Framing
Santa Fe, NM
505.984.1007

Shorty's Caboy Hattery
shortyshattery.com

Star York
staryorksculpture.com

Teal Blake
tealblake.com

Wahoo! Santa Fe
wahoosantafe.com

Wendy McEahern
wmphotosantafe.com

University of Virginia (1998). *Eastward Ho! The Dude Ranch Hits the Trail 1925-1955*. From the American Studies Program.

Framing by **Perspectives Fine Art Framing, Santa Fe**

Cowboy hats by **Shorty's Caboy Hattery**

All other scarves and other props from the collection of **Wahoo! Santa Fe**

SCARVES COURTESY OF:

Buckeye Blake, pages 104, 105

Buckeye Blake and Alan Chadwick, page 106

Carla Liesen and David Holl, pages 110, 111

Donna Howell-Sickles, page 112

Jack Pressler, pages 52, 53, 73, 136 (bottom)

James Mann, page 12

Sally "Cookie Mom" Smith and Alan Chadwick, pages 114, 115

Teal Blake, pages 107, 108, 109

UNTIL WE MEET AGAIN

Now the shadows 'cross the valley
They flee the setting sun
As they lengthen into twilight
The stars awaken one by one
And these songs we share between us
Remain to warm the night
Like old friends and weary travelers
In lingering firelight

Happy trails and lucky travels
To you, the best of friends
Though tomorrow finds us parted
I'll leave these words where memory wends
May your laughter lighten hard times
And smile soften the rain
And may a song your pathway brighten
Until we meet again

c. 1996 Wily Western Music BMI
Wily Jim Pfeiffer / Used by permission

Diane Zamost owns Wahoo! Santa Fe, a store that sells both vintage and new western wear. For more than twenty years, she has been buying and selling western wear at horse shows, rodeos, western music and poetry gatherings, and anywhere else people appreciate cowboy couture. People visit her store from all over the world to bask in the nostalgia of the romantic West. She lives in Santa Fe.

Wendy McEahern is a commercial, editorial, and fine art photographer known for her meticulous lighting, creative collaboration with clients, and enthusiasm in tackling difficult subjects. Her work has appeared in catalogs, advertisements, and magazines, including *Trend*, the *Santa Fean, Southwest Art, Art in America, Native Peoples,* and the *Essential Guide*. A longtime Santa Fe resident, she shares her home and garden with her cats, Rumi and Xochi. To see more of her work, visit her website at wmphotosantafe.com.